IN THE CURRENT WHERE DROWNING IS BEAUTIFUL

ABIGAIL CHABITNOY

in the current
where drowning
is beautiful

Wesleyan University Press / Middletown, Connecticut

Wesleyan University Press
Middletown CT 06459
www.wesleyan.edu/wespress
2022 © Abigail Kerstetter
Manufactured in the United States of America
Library of Congress Cataloging-in-Publication Data

Names: Chabitnoy, Abigail, author.
Title: In the current where drowning is beautiful / Abigail Chabitnoy.
Other titles: In the current where drowning is beautiful (Compilation)
Description: Middletown, CT: Wesleyan University Press, [2022] |
    Series: Wesleyan poetry | Summary: "Award-winning poet interweaves English and
    Alutiiq as a response to the colonial violence and the silencing of indigenous women,
    in particular the crisis of missing and murdered indigenous women and girls"
    —Provided by publisher.
Identifiers: LCCN 2022013698 (print) | LCCN 2022013699 (ebook) |
    ISBN 9780819500120 (hardcover) | ISBN 9780819500137 (paperback) |
    ISBN 9780819500144 (ebook)
Subjects: LCSH: Indigenous peoples—Poetry. | LCGFT: Poetry.
Classification: LCC PS3603.H315 I5 2022 (print) | LCC PS3603.H315 (ebook) |
    DDC 811/.6—dc23/eng/20220517
LC record available at https://lccn.loc.gov/2022013698
LC ebook record available at https://lccn.loc.gov/2022013699

5 4 3 2 1

CONTENTS

～

～

～

~

~

~

IN THE CURRENT WHERE DROWNING IS BEAUTIFUL

∼

I am looking for a way to sound
     the women catch / in my throat
     water
               lung

How do you say the women are at the beach?,
     wave after wave
standing on shore
still?,
the water now to our throats   looking
for a wavesend where otherwise
     a field fallows—

Listen, they cut my fingers fin, fine, finé my neck gilled slit so I too could
breathe and became aware another tongue carried
in my throat

There was earth at the bottom so I dug
There was a sea and a knife and a sacrifice
     and looking back
I drank, salt and all
     the words I am learning

WAVE. moving swell on the surface. a disturbance that carries energy. *swell.*

see also, wave function. waves in phase, with like signs, will interfere constructively, leading to the possibility of bonding. those out of phase, with unalike signs, will interfere destructively.

we were unable to head for shore
*since we would be rolled over by the **swell**—*

SIGNS YOU ARE STANDING AT THE END

Two-thirds of the country is in drought. The waters have all gone walking.

Nunakuarluni.[1]

When white peaks crested the rolling hills behind our house

I knew it was time.

We understand since we are children waves break waves travel waves do the wave. Did the wave make it across the room? Did the people who started it move across the room?

Cause of death: traumatized. Cause of death: bad heart. Cause of death: exposure.[2]

(I heard it was an accident. In the end. In the breakers. There was no boat when I heard it.)

I took my sister and some others out the back door. The calm was not and the neatly kept lawn was not.

The sleeper wave was not.

Too many teeth I saw too late. The wave would not be dove under.

It turned snow, wet and heaving and we
                                were already running.

---

[1] Take

[2] to the cold air; to want of sea ice; to warming air; to a landscape without trees; too many ribs;
    to the sea; to ghosts; to loss
                of stable earth to plant one's feet, one's seed, one's egg, one's teeth.

~c

After, a field. I could hear every dead thing.

How do we behave in the field?

They asked for a story, the ones we'd have to leave behind. Swallowed
by the hoary mouth.
Never ignore what someone tells you in a dream, once the women said.
You are trying to remember what someone said
who is dead.

Quliyangua'uciikamken.[3] —

Laam'paaq kuarsgu.[4]

---

[3] I will tell you a story
[4] hard to leave in good light

IN THE FIELD

They asked me if I was a citizen.

They wanted to know what I had seen/
I had heard/
this was only a test:

Look at the mark and tell them what you see.

⁓

Akarngasqangcugmek pilirluku,[1]
a woman said to me.

They want more,
she said.

I gave her a tooth from my mouth
to cut the skin stretched before her.

She dug. With her mouth
she dug enough holes
in the earth she divided
with her work.

She cut the skin even
into pieces she divided
in the earth:

>   this is for your mouth
>   this is for your stomach
>   this is for your hand
>   this is for your rib
>   this is for your table
>   this is for sharing
>   this is for later
>   this is for the others
>   this
>   is (for) you

For each she wound a thread
around my neck.

⌣

I see a well,
I said.

I showed them my hands
clean under the nails and
open
    swallowed the dirt
under my tongue.

They let me walk away

with the needle
in my eye.

They don't look you
in the eyes, these men
                these days.

I walked away with a garden
in my throat and seeds
on my tongue.

---

[1] Make a way, make your way. dot by dot, string around your waist

A PERSISTENT DREAM OF LARGE BODIES

for Joan, and those she is called after

Naviyuk   how to tell you
last night we were on this ship together
and you were there to comfort me?

But this morning I am afraid for you
       black steeling over the waters.

My lips are never not split

                splitting—

Tell me, are the wolves living
along this shoreline any gentler
than the Moscow water dog?

Even the promyshlenniki let them go
extinct.

Have we ever not been readying for war
in your lifetime?

Already my family is calling me—

      the ones I don't know
      how to name,

   ⌣

           In the stories I learned as a girl
           you are otherwise called
           after one who knows things.

           You are called after one who knows
           how to listen.

           She was given fire and earth.

This ground we are on has a history
of flooding:

    does it follow we are drowning?

Cut the breast out of a woman and she becomes a bird.
Or was it her guts?

She can fly, I mean. It's that simple. So the stories go.

Girls go into the woods and return mothers
so we invent little men, irresistible magic.

Have we ever not been readying for war?

At any moment the ship could sink: mothers go into the water
become forces to be reckoned—

It can all fail tragically.

The waters take
and give us back our dead.

We will have this ship
the water, contents we have found.

ANATOMY OF A WAVE

It had everything and nothing to do
with mettle
     fire before flint before,

How many bodies will a lead ball move
     through?

How many can one stand in a row?

    When the tide went out, they had nowhere to run
       but that was many years ago, and if they have not died they live
happily still.
          But you and I know that's not how the story goes.

I wake more ghosts each morning:
           when I was born my mother and father
           planted a tree west of the garden.

           We ripped it out when I left home—
           its roots never took,
           its limbs harbored mold in the sticky east wind.

We used to think a weak spine
was inherited
         but consider the shark
         how some will stop swimming
         in their sleep.

How does the forecast change?

We make weather with our teeth.
Why should I be afraid of the sea?
Let the toothed skin lie
     if it asks too many bones.

Wait for the waves
        to start skipping,

Tie down the drifters and stretch the stomach before the fall.

Don't turn your back on the water.

What else grows on an island
                without trees?

    The need to make
makes body—

                                    Others have seen water act this way before,
                                            it was many years ago,
                                    how many bodies a single wave can carry,
                                        how many relatives, casually.

                        They tied their boats to the tops of trees
                                so the water wouldn't lose them,
                                        so the story goes.

Some say it was a boat that killed them. Bad heart, *traumatized*. Accidently.
I'm telling you what happens. She missed the boat.

Imagine what it might be like
                when the waters come
to be a fish
                to be twelve strong, to be six, two hundred, or forty
                sharks swimming toward you—

ALL THE DAUGHTERS

Liminally fault or cause,
each morning and most afternoons
brush against the moon,

knock from its axis, remember,

I keep living because someone else does not.

Do the fish in the desert share the shore's vertigo?

What does water know of the want
of our hands?

You think it's just shallow, but

if a man or a woman is sucked into the mudflats where
before they were treading leisurely

(the water or the dirt)
if too cold to say it was leisurely (the man, the woman, or the water)
but rather it wasn't certain they were drowning

is it my fault they are there?

Sea change, a grey, another father, another daughter swept
in the current. (see *Fault/line (disambiguation)*; see *fracture* or *crevice/
crevasse*)

The water is trending higher these days with or without
my paper moon and the wings in my corner are just
for holding detritus.

The cat's cradle hanging from the ceiling is a hazard, sure,
but only if you come at it from the wrong angle, the work
or the moon.

Rivers string through maps through days
through lips slipped grit

(we keep living—),

And if each of these beings has agency (such as the dirt)
you can hardly blame yourself if the tide goes out and they're left
sticks in the mud

        —unless of course you have a boat and saw
them struggling when there was still water enough
to swim.

How will you spin it?

> In August, girls sing songs and weave string figures
> to tangle the legs of the sun and slow its departure
> for winter. I would let go the sun for a fish or a bird
> to carry all the daughters across, and yes, the fathers
> and the mothers and the sons,

    how far have you had to run?

The question to ask in such times is not why they jumped
when the water was cold, what drew two bodies apart
in the first place,
        the nature of the agency, the use
                of flapping.

Shorelines can be-witch like that: we all want to be seen
to shine.

IN THE CURRENT WHERE DROWNING IS BEAUTIFUL

White breaks first, waves
green,   then black
shining seas   ships sailing
not sailing:
what is still
wanting wind.

Used to be no man could go against,
this weather too will pass. The wind
not a river.

And if a puddle at the last
gives way
to desert:
corked bottle
walled city
veiled woman,

buried one, were you afraid?
Carwaq tukniuq.[1]

If air the conscious element—
sometimes breath
sometimes bird—

the last few days have been windy, but

The current is strong, Nikifor,
and it rains all the time.

Tamiinek taangaq aturtapet,[2]

---

[1] There is a river of woe, and a river to forget, and then there is the river
that does not break by all the gods.

[2] Good to the last drop.

and sometimes
if I were not afraid,
a fish
with teeth
after all.

SUPPLEMENTAL ENRICHMENT CURRICULUM

As children,
we learned the names
for all the pieces of
a boat named *Mimi* and how
to safely dispel salt from the sea
water in a pinch
assuming the presence
of a black plastic bag,
enough vessels
to be filled.

We learned how to warm a man
who had slipped in the water
how to make him tick
again—how to regulate the heart
again—how to make it race
again.
We learned it was
a vulnerable thing—the man,
muscle, the heart.

By summer we forgot
in absence of a vessel to name
the scarcity of shores
to claim
hemmed in
by our green lawns and sated
by the bottled water
in our second fridges.

We didn't learn to identify
how long a body had come
by the rivers where we drew
the line.

We didn't learn to wash our wounds
to keep flesh eaters at bay.

We didn't learn the many ways
water knew we would have
to thirst

    the many ways our bodies
    would be found and filled
    wanting.

We didn't learn where to find a branch
unblooded that would hold us
when there were no more boats
when the waters began to rise
and the rivers took back their own.

Man-eating monsters exist
through every body of water
in the imagination at least

Let this   , body
                    bear stones
on the other side   of
the flood—

                    Body,
              forever / still
                    trying
              to decide
        (/how) to lay down
                    these arms

        When their weight
                demands
              to be upheld

        When their comfort-
              plus depends on
              my complexion
or
              not least my
come(-when-called-)liness
        my propensity for lines
              in which to stand
              my complicit course
                    of inaction

        Someday-daughter,
              how you sit or
                    don't sit
        can make waves

Ears turn to war on the shore
line
bank unyielding
distilled before the break—

I am contemplating words that take the shape
of O

moon
crater
face
sole-made boat
body in water
descending
tooth
hem
mother
open hand
closed fist
site of (dis)articulation

Every kind (of) red mouth

IF A FIELD

            very well. Crack open my ribs and crawl my chest. Make of me one
you can live with—
                Only this too: how we (be)have in the field
I may stand her(e) until I am down to waist and I will not
get used to that smile, wide-eyed because you've never seen the hole you laid down in.

It rains, and we use the water in everything.

~

the men wanted to play jungle but
they didn't know how / to assuage the tyger.

my teeth broke in half and i cut myself
on my own sharpness.

they laughed as they poured out the water.
we watched as they poured out the water.
i watched as they poured out the water.

each day i pour out the water.

it wears a body down / these games
ware bodies mothers ware
children ware war
                    the bodies wear(y)

looking for my contents.

iqallut tuqumaut.

allrani suu'ut caqainek pukugtaartut.

skuunaq tang'rk'gka.

agyat unugmi antaartut.

WAVELENGTH. the distance between the crests of two waves.

it's the interaction of wave swell with the current
the curved—curving—current narrowly focuses the wave's energy
                    *shortens their **wavelengths** and makes them steep/er*

the wavelength can always be determined by measuring the distance between
any two corresponding points on adjacent waves.

LIGHT TRIPTYCH

I.

Let's begin again.

It was dark in the wolf.
It was dark in the whale.
            in the shark.

It was dark at the bottom
            of the sea
            where they threw the girl
            with no one.
            where they threw the girl
            who did not wish to marry.

It was dark in the girl.

Are you surprised? Bright lights still
cast shadows.

It was dark in the wolf, in the whale, in the shark.
It was dark in the sea, in the girl.
Except behind her sister's teeth, when she opened her mouth to speak.

II.

The rules of the game are simple
my brother's girl explained.

She shined her light straight
in my eye:

When you see it take it,
shine for the next
to see.

III.

I dreamt my teeth fell by the road.
They were loose and I pulled and I left
them fall.

You convinced me to leave them
where they lay
          where I had dropped them—

It was too late to turn around
you said

It was too late when I realized
there were no others
behind them

We continued down the road
without teeth

She drank from the river
the girl left behind

She drank from the river
until she could bend
trees lay their trunks
over the water

She drank from the river
until she had her fill
of shine

KINGUGTURNINGAITUA[1]

What if we were born with skin thick
and hard as teeth?

And every time another one of us was thrown into the sea
we became a wondrous beast?

A 22 foot, 20,000 pound, 50-year-old-mother-to-be
Carcharodon carcharias[2]
Qilalugaq Qirniqtaq[3]
Monodon monoceros[4]
"The one of the depth of the sea"
"The one who did not wish to mother"
"Giver of strength"—

There once was a man
who was ravenous.

There once was a rainbow-colored man-worm
who was ravenous.

With the face of a man, the body of a worm
many human feet and towards the end an eagle's talons
the ravenous one devoured everything it encountered.

Only a spiritually powerful hunter
was able to kill the beast.

A spiritually powerful hunter
was able to kill the beast.

---

[1] I won't swallow the worm
[2] but the sharp-toothed one
[3]   "black fish"
[4]   with one tooth and one horn—

～

Or the shark could be just
a shark otherwise a snake or
a ravenous man and/or the women
could just be
discards
       overboard.

At least in my dream
they were shining.

Still, I won't take the bait
in my mouth—

Iksak ipegtuq.[5]
Iqsak una nenermek pilimauq.[6]
Iqsak cukingq'rtuq.[7]

Kingugturningaitua.[8]
[I will put the bait on my hook.][9]

---

[5] The fishhook is sharp
[6]   bone
[7]   (and) barbed
[8] [ ] won't take the worm in my mouth
[9] (when) I take the bait on your hook

BAPTISM BY FIRE

After the painting Baptism by Fire *(2010), by John Patrick Cobb,*
displayed at the Mexic-Arte Museum in Austin, Texas

In a painting in the tent
        did they call it shrine?
        did they call it temple?
in the museum in the part of Texas
        everyone said was all right
        everyone said would be alright

I found a girl with my mother's name
        who brought fire down from
the mountains.

It would have been dark without it
don't you think? the sky
        burdened with gold
but for that woman-sized break of blue
she passed through.

        She carried this fire from the gods
          or the heavens
          or the mountains
       in her dress—

       in the earth
      on the ground
       at her feet

       that is,
         out of her hands
       it would have cast the setting
         in shadow.

Sometimes you have to rip a hole
in the sky.

Sometimes you have to tear a seam
into the fabric:

> This is my beloved Mother
> no one told to put the fire down,
>
> This my beloved mother
> no one cast her glow into shadow and
> shame.
>
> This is my beloved Mother
> with fire in her dress,
> see: She prepares to ignite the fire
> with her magic.

CAMOUFLAGE, DEFENSE, AND PREDATION
BEING AMONG THE REASONS

fish are thought to emit their own light,
talk to your future daughter as though nothing is wrong.

Or, if you want her to be strong and able to adapt in ways
that haven't been found out yet
                              tell her everything.

Apologize if you think it will help
or don't. It will be too late—

        unarmed boys and fathers, even mothers, even girls will be dead.
you were afraid. someone you loved was afraid. someone you
would distance yourself from entirely was afraid.

And that person who was afraid had too many arms
and the person they feared had none.   *See the shining sea?*

Tell her you are working on her birthday
present as if this day will arrive. Tell her it will
save her life.

You still have time to figure it out.

Not arms. There will be enough, even if she is born without any.
Not legs. There will be enough crossed, and not enough dry land.

How would you feel about an extra heart? My own a hole
into each of you pour. The usual number of ribs to encase it
and no more. But it can hold more than it looks outside.

This hole is where you can throw your own children
when you can no longer feed them and their last tooth breaks on the rocks
they were sucking and the air above thins, grows warm.

The tundra begins to thaw. Hell breaks loose.

A sports drink company has made the first man out of water
and isn't it a good time to be alive? one shines briefly

Unless of course you are the water
                              or the man,

One dies soon.

                              What if we skip to the end? I'll make you half fish and
                                                        luminous.

I sometimes feel with my mother we
are nestled in the hand of god only god
                              is female and in her hand is a hole
                              we must pass through to be caught
to feed the men again and again
                              to feed the women and the children
and the men—

And it's not personal, or it is, but the hand is thinking
of closing. I think the hand is closing.

                    After all, you can only throw a fish so many times
              before *bad heart*, before *traumatized*, before it looks like a world
                                        with a lot of dead women.

Daughter in this dream I stood before the water until mud. One
by one my teeth fell out and rolled into the sand and my glowing bones
parted ways suggesting small boats
                              each a wave carried back to sea.

HOLES IN THE FIELD

The women are not there.

The girls are not there.

What if the sea were a mouth
                                a neck
opening?

> *Imam taanga taryutuu'uq.*[1]

Empty.

Full.

Otherwise, "*imaq.*"

Otherwise, "a liquid contained inside."

"Contents"
                rising.

Take care, each
point of stress.

The word for the week is *Woman. Arnat peknartutaartut.*[2]

This is only a test: how closely are you listening?

We must dive.

---

[1]   salt
[2] women harden

Everywhere to wash
my hands
      there was blood.

  Back bending
        we dove

the words air in our throats.

Without them you are not a whole person,
Emaq said to me at the grave.

WHEN YOU SAY THE DEER
SWEPT OUT TO SEA WAS 'SAVED'

to amass
to deposit
to heap
to hoard
to invest
[a] hill
to lay aside
to lay away
to keep
to deliver
to take
to economize
to redeem
to tender

Ayaquq egtaakait cuumi.[1]

a marginal propensity [to save]
(a neck)
[possibly an] egg
a stitch in time saves nine

(to snatch)

[one requires] the ark
[otherwise a] flotation device
([a] Noah)
a people saved is a land earned
([a] reserve)

---

[1] They used to throw a harpoon before. As a drag on the wound(ed).
To make the animal visible in the water.

your hide or theirs
your peach
your pinch
your stone

the key to
the human race
with the help of
the day god
killer
king
know it all—

Know it all.

HOW ABOUT A UNICORN HORN?

Impatient, restless, unrelenting—
I would like to dream more often
wonderful beasts than war.

Or an ordinary tooth: Mother
plait my hair and send me
to the sea, let me be
unseen.

Wicked women are allowed as much
and I am tired of being easy
prey.

How many times have I woke
unable to scream?
mouth agape and filling
with air—

I used to
at first
that is
thought it strange
to dream a man
didn't know
and know
he meant to
do me
wrong.

The dream is a reliable indicator
She is waking up.

The dream is a harbinger often
She is waking up.

The dream is a situation increasing
She is waking up.

There were tines strewn across the bed
I woke, woke with my hand in a fist
around a bloodied
hollow
point.

IF YOU'RE GOING TO LOOK LIKE A WOLF THEY HAVE TO LOVE YOU MORE THAN THEY FEAR YOU

The first deer had large teeth and no horns
and were not afraid.

The first deer did not have enough fear
for the men who needed them
to survive.

A woman decided to let the men eat
a grandmother decided her deer shall have horns
and be afraid
someone's mother decided the men shall eat
and shall be feared.

⌒

A man thought wolves should be used
to cull the herd.

And we who had been catching water
dripping through stone
in the homes we dug
out of the earth
we licked our
long teeth
clean

and set to work.

~

when i grew sick on cakes and sweet
meats i left / home

rain in my gaping and
memory of water turning
my lungs

i broke down in the desert
where border
men held

fire broke

i stayed with the women
i found
       wanting to see a miracle
           a wall
                turn water
          what remained
after a flood

who could stand upright
which fish could survive it
which birds would return
                branches in their clutch
to light upon

WAVE CREST. the top of a wave.

point of maximum displacement. during storms
the wave heights
increase.

(her) **crest** rose
                and
        fell—

SWELL

We took the long way to pick raspberries and find
the old grave

weathered crosses and men young
from mining years

before the ground was thawed.

⌣

Glaciers give their own warning. Ice
                        on the margins
cracks under our weight.

⌣

The more distance between
the mountains grew. It used to be the river

channeled the other side but lately
banks are breaking.

The high ground isn't.

Many areas have seen disappearances
glaciers and ice sheets and rivers
short of the sea—

the face never the same.

⌣

Suppose somebody would have made the spotted feather into bedding,
isn't most of our armor against cold these days?

I was thinking of a hat in need of a feather or two
        or

sharper a mask when the men broke through
the trees
        trying to be small.

Am I predator or prey
they didn't see me? And they?

That they are not spirits is certain. That my coat is not thick enough
to be still is apparent. The cold get under my skin.

        Not bear or fox. I've never seen a wolf
        in the wild.

⁓

They found Ashley before I left.
Before that they found Olivia.

⁓

With the necks of 200 birds I could have made a garment
capable of these surroundings

if good enough for the sea. The mothers
would give them stories, stories, stories.

The children would watch, listen and learn.

        But there's the rope   the web
with its too-large
               holes.

My families don't tell stories, so
      we must use the net. *Kugyaq atuk'gka.*[1]

---

[1] (to secure the ocean floor)

~

One, one thousand, two thousand, three thousand, four thousand still
waiting to be found.

> *Amlertut nuumiRat kalikami.*[2]
> *Amlertut paniyat kalikami.*[3]
> *Amlertut alqat kalikami.*[4]
> *Amlertut maamat kalikami.*[5]
> *Amlertut arnat kalikami.*[6]

Keep counting.

~

> The woman was full of rage.
> The woman was full of vengeance.
> The woman moved mountains and grew islands in the sea.
>
> The woman was beautiful so beautiful
> the cormorants decided to mate with her.
>
> They changed shapes and took turns breeding with the woman
> and flew away
>
> and later when the woman had birthed
> all the children the cormorants carried them in their mouths
> like seed and sowed them all over the world.
>
> Does it follow each violent act bears fruit?

~

---

[2] there are lots of numbers on the paper
[3] there are lots of paper daughters
[4] there are lots with sisters
[5] there are lots with mothers
[6] there are Lots
    razed with women

43

I'm supposed to have astonishing heat in my blood but
think it's all been let by now.

Buildings are still dangerous
to enter.

Unsafe structures and
openings may be present.

The white dog's teeth left my coat whole but the skin
was broken underneath.

Guard the slow heat from the wound.

⌣

I want to tell you too it is beautiful, the walls here
their own shade of green where the ice is thin
blue becomes its own north light,   but

human qualities are most evident
in the lines we cut.

The face falls. They don't grow back.[7]

These openings are old and unmaintained
                                        may be
without breathable air.

Do not attempt to go under. Do not attempt to go back
wards.

Keep counting.

The melt deep and wilding.

---

[7] glaciers, or—

QULIYANGUA'UCIIKAMKEN[1]

I am afraid of most waters but some days
   desire drowning—
                  drop my eye
below the sight.

                      "Hello blackwater."

   wish some days
to put on my sister's skin
                  to see the body
other than my death.

What if this river is wind? I don't really know
about sharks and salmon after all.

     swim. not swim. one must take care
     entering any body of modest depth.

I will tell you a story,

more mouth than maw these days
more bird than fish—

What we're missing, waves: an exact measurement
of distance
               a body in context
               an appreciation for the size
of a full grown walrus.

One dies soon.

                    It used to be these events occurred
                        hundreds of years
                              apart.

---

[1] Let me tell you—

The story goes and grows until no bigger than a harbor
seal,
      small and
                          spotted
in need of saving and   native
          to the wrong waters.

Blackwater, bad weather,
How do you know if you're holding walrus
elephant
        deer   or girl?
           snow or
ash?

What if this wind is a river?

Yaatiini, akgua'aq, ernerpak cali aqllangenguartuq.[2]

---

[2] by the sea, wash your hair

REDIRECTION WITH MY DEAD RELATIVES

Nikifor i need you to hear me
in my family we don't tell stories

list the living & dead
faces know(n) & unknown
ask to be blessed

at the end of our memories/
cut the rhyme short

the way we were taught
to ready ourselves for night
to not teach us
to [say] *die* or *take.*

Nikifor i need you to bear the birds
need you to bear the burden
of You because *ilat naata allringumi ell'uteng*[1]
but positing between
home & post-home

over & again, again
has made this body [a] rupture

i don't remember the list
taught to carry these days
being honest
i'm afraid to be alone/outside
night.

Nikifor i must speak to you
a woman grown [&/] afraid
to be myself outside when
dark.

We call water too: a body
contained inside, and if ruptured
[then/at] least, i am many::

each grave, each girl-shape|d (each) hole ((each))
a boat named for those called
and calling—

<hr>

[1] we remain, we should

SHE IS MAKING ROPE

Call it a mess.
Call it a [geological] mess.
Call it a[n historical] mess.
Call it a current
event,
Body a continent
        curved
    broken
        stacked
under the heel of a pre-
Columbus
        boot.

You think he was the first?

Birdsong to the preconditioned ear a precursor
to the kind/of curses bundled
finer than spindle/
these days—
                that the woman should not know
she has been abused
until there are twins with her own eyes
and someone else's mouth and ears.

She wouldn't go quietly into the earth   *there will always be wicked men and*
to fire, to dark after dark.   *weary women*

It's not true what they say about fish
in/the sea these days
                        looks like a world with a lot
of dead women, these days
even the birds are at risk.

Who's vindictive now? Bury the branch
we can't have for our own.

In decline: sea ice, insects, bearded seals, young
whales, martens on the Oregon coast. Giraffes

hum to each other
through the night
no one noticed:

ARaʃkumek piliyuq.[1]

Different ways to say the same thing :: Still
she has some uses, still/she may have some resources
still she may be ravaged,

                    her

        and all her

              pieces—   *(separate the part from*
                                                                    the whole, twist and braid

Adria, are you lost yet? Hum   *the line long for casting)*
this humming too
a line to bind
            to follow when the shore departs.

When vision is impaired we/sound
the other to keep the herd
together—
          her, and all her pieces.

---

[1] with the thread, that which we always use
when we sew, with the thread
around my neck   the woman wrapped—
she is making rope.

I.

I'd want you to be a girl, even now.
Ashley-Olivia-Akelina-Nikifor—you would have
too many names to go missing.

Once there was and once there was not
a brass bed in the woods
glass that didn't cut your feet and
feet that cut like glass
once there was enough coral in the sea
to make a kingdom
once there was a wolf
on the way to grandma's house and
when she told you stories
the moon shone from her mouth
against the dark lining
the sunken earth.

Youngest daughter, would you have liked the one
about the sea women?
                                    understand when I tell you
no heaven or man is enough
to buy your silence?

Or is this how you begin 300 years
in purgatory?
                    vindictive or   entombed

They will tell you to smile.
Guard your tongue with teeth.

II.

John says he is listening to your concerns.

8-year-old Franklin of Guatemala was
reunited with his father and watching them
embrace right now it is possible to forget
the latest counts

250 or 559 or more than 400
at least 2,000[1]   (maybe 14,000)[2]
186, or more than 10,000[3]
500 or 2,000   as many as 15,000[4]
btw 200 or 300 and 500, or 2,000[5]

Jakelin-Albertha-Savanna-

colonies of birds are already in decline. cite predation.[6]

(alternatively, such facts vary—by the time you read this we will have forgotten how many. the list grows. but who's counting?)

     and yes I
can still cry while showing you
my teeth,   but
     I couldn't tell you why I feel
vertigo
   in the bed
 in the house where
      I
was a child
   only,

---

[1] separated.
[2] detained.
[3] buried.
[4] missing. murdered. prone
[5] to be incorrectly labeled.
[6] massacred

This is America and it is (year-of-our-supposed-lord) ___.
This is America since 1492.
This is America, we were born taking children from their mothers and their fathers.
This is America and we've been taking babies from mothers with too many babies
(I.Y.O.) in your lifetime.
This is America and I want to tell you too it is beautiful

                                                        but
                            —vindictive or entombed—

Now we are sending soldiers to the mothers with their children fleeing soldiers
we inspired to threaten mothers with their children.

Still we are burying women with their mouths closed.
Still we are buying women with our mouths closed.

Still we are missing.

III.

Not all the children have come home not all the children come home not all the
children are children get to be children will have children

IV.

"Yeah, well, [kids]* get stolen. That's how it goes."

        *he might have said "land." he might have said "women." he might have been
        smiling respectfully to diffuse the situation.

V.

A snake-body-water once told me girls
who get carried away like that are capable of
changing into birds
why not fish as well or
wolves come to that
if you're going to leave her body in
a sunken state
after all I'm not the first
to tell stories about wolves
in the water.

VI.

The first deer had large teeth and no horns and
were not afraid.

Water drips through stone.

Girls get thrown from the boat
become witches in need of a good comb.

So the story goes
how it goes.

There is in many a hungry one
inside.

The men give each other warning and
in this they are fair:

if the sea witch appear before you
best tuck your tail and run.

VII.

What if *Sherry* you were a seed?
What if *Ariel* you were a woman
for the end and beginning
the world?

Now you put on your extra skin
now you take out your extra teeth
wash the blood in the high tide.

VIII.

Women were killed

> "by fire, by water, by hanging in air, burying in earth,
> by asphyxiation, penetration, striking, piercing, crushing
> in a thousand
> and one ways."

You forgot exposure (which *Patricia* knows in Montana may include stabbing).

IX.

The first deer had large teeth and no horns and
were not afraid.

X.

Now you don't see us
Now you don't

I'm not going to play
your blackout games

but know:

my teeth still shine
in the dark.

a body buried still
speaks.

above or
below

don't imagine there is nothing at the bottom.

SHE THOUGHT THIS MIGHT BE HOW IT ENDS

I thought I should be able to make a day hour utter
a word but then
out of time / of
language / wanting
to know how to say
who my relatives are.

This week: The ball is round.
Mayaciik akagngauq. The ball is round.

You get a thing that is round
a word / the wor(l)d
is round.

These days, no small feat. Only hands.
Will you hold the round thing in your hands
even if they are small   and wearing holes?

How do you know there aren't men without
hearts with heads in their chest? Mouth
where stomach.

Sometimes the wife-sister is clever and sometimes
she helps her husband-brother(s) but
in most of the stories she is expendable

if not disposed entirely.

I wanted to show the heron to the lake / or
the crane
          but it was gone.

The loon gave the [girl] sight / so
the [girl] gave the loon [her] white breast.

The man killed all the girl's relatives / so
They were gone / so
the man killed the girl.

Or did the girl kill the man? Whose story is this
again?

I don't know how to say I know who my relatives are.

I don't.

THE WORD OF THE WEEK IS WAVE

How do you say *a wave that eats people*?
How do you say *a wave that consumes us*?
How do you say *a wave capable of carrying us away*?
How do you say *a wave is capable*?
How do you say *a wave is culpable*?

The water's waking up. *Qangyut angtaartut,*[1]
   compounded by our fetch.

How do you measure the distance
between *us* and *not us*?

You can't make big waves in a small pond
however hard or long the wind blows
   but you can break a body
of water open with enough change
in the atmosphere.

Still, a good woman should be fetching
   that's what you told us—
bottle fetching in small vessels.

Scarcity drives the market:
let me share with you my unbottled fetch
and let it be abounding.

If a modest wind blows over
water uninterrupted for hundreds of
miles—

How do you say *a people that is culpable*?
How do you say *a people that is capable*?

---

[1] we pitch and swell,

Nuna ushnertuq.[2]
Heavy rains wash away a little then
a little more.

Records tend to scarcity. *Qayaq miktuq.*[3]

Grandmothers, tell your granddaughters
stories

how your grandmothers survived.

---

[2] the land sinks:
[3] a kayak is smaller still than an ark, by degrees

~

a tree with all its branches cut becomes otherwise a spike.

though i agree, a body shouldn't bear so many arms.

what if instead a landscape with no trees?

what if a body   too cold to cross in one's own skin?

what if wind so fierce you could not go against it? what if that wind held you
at arms length
                    and someone—a brave (man or) woman—paddled into that wind, to
the source, and found there a puffed up man sitting on a cliff blowing violently?

i was dreaming it would be fine weather tomorrow,

                    he shot the man, who retreated but did not die. she searched out other winds and stuffed their
mouths with earth. these noble actions calmed the winds but did not tame them permanently.

we're in the fall now. what will you do when that body swells? when that body rises and
comes to you?

how else will you secure your weight on a spike when the sea settles where the sea must be?

standing on that shore without arms
looking out all the shining bodies
                                        only carrion birds to carry your blooded olive branch

WAVE HEIGHT. the distance between a wave's crest and trough.

the significant **wave height** *is the average . . . [and] occur[ed] over a given period.*

Build safer ships.

I TOO GROW TIRED OF THE PLOT

The wind is not a river
Someday
It will end

The river or
The wind—
Can't recall

If we give the river rights
Any person
Must have seen
She is vulnerable

We must have seen
The end

Hot air blows
Unconcerned by persons
Raising the likelihood of
Drought
       So they say

How does the river fare?

I guess it's true
Women are still talking about weather
One can't be too careful
With the currents
These days

Once there was a river with 134 ribbons in her hair

The river gives up
The ghost

Once there was a beautiful river
Maligned for her long hair

These days the river thinks
She would like to be more
      Or moored

When she left there was no more water
For drinking or for washing
When she left there were no more fish
Bones in the mud in place of ribbons

These days the river likes to think
We all wash out in the sea

The soles she kept of each shoe
collected on her shores
caught in her knotted hair
she held aloft and fixed
a ribbon to each small vessel

These days the river thinks
are overdue for a flood.

A FOUR-PART APOLOGY FOR MY CONTINUED BEING

I hear you think   I'm a witch or
your word for   witch.

Is it the finger or the mark I am
posit(ion)ing?

Did you hear the one about the man who was envied
above all men
                he was turned into a white-faced bear   then
he became a white-faced bear.

I used to think the beach was safe
but lately
        they say bears are going back to the island
despite the distance growing,

                         rising seas and all—

The fish are less abundant these days
soon that thing you like to say   (speaking here now
about fish in the sea   to the more general
when someone doesn't like you back   you)
               won't be true.

It's been awhile since they were
large enough to feed a crowd with as few as seven
                  and
bears are not people after all:

if that bear was a man once you must see
he's something more now
                and if that bear was a woman
haven't you known: she's nursed such hunger all her life?
and before that?

since the beginning—
                        Later locals blame
an abundance of cattle.

        ～

So, finger or mark? I wear a new ring with that shovel
full of stars
                bogged in jet, and guess

I'm trying to say again I wanted this to be beautiful
how you could almost think they were
campfires in the Badlands instead of greased holes
sinking the earth

                too small for my thumb.

        ～

I used to think they were stars in the field
or doe eyes—
                not the ones in headlights   but
                the kind that don't know they're in danger

don't know they're meant to run,

maybe pearls in the ocean
when the sun lights the waves just right

(there had to be enough somewhere
to string all those pretty necks)

and all this time just another familiar   "by fire, by water
cycle, as violent—   by hanging in air ..."

        ～

In my other hand the waves are red so
very well, I'll tell you a story for the end.

It starts at the beginning. An island
precludes a sea and all my babies before me

learned to swim before they were born
to test these waters.

Nothing can prepare you for being
swallowed whole:

    instinct kicks in,
     hold your breath and
wait to be released.

   ~c

Angayuk,[1] how to tell you
I left you there
   where the ship is sinking or
the water rising
      or on an island with cattle
     lowing, still
digging holes in the earth.

Breathing is a costly act.

———————

[1] Like a friend, or sister; one who connects us elsewhere, to facilitate movement—of selves, resources,
and goods; of mooring in times of need

URIITARSURCIQUA

I was looking for a shell
for a house to keep
   in my pockets
small enough to hold onto
but large enough to fit
         my hips   (or
was it   my lips?

what story doesn't fill
with holes?)

uriitarsurciqua[1]

curved on one side
flat on the other
like a boat—

I wanted it to be blue
for my mother I suppose
         (the house)
I wanted my mother
    to approve

(in this telling even the mice
are spared—they floated
across the water and became
stuck on rocks
they became *uriitat*[2]—they didn't
drown, though children
these days
eat them raw)

but each one I found already
was living and
I dropped all the pieces
that moved.

---

[1] I am going to get some bidarkies—
[2] chiton, otherwise composed in the shape of a traditional skin/ boat.

When we were children
we had four hermit crabs and my sister
killed two.

She threw them against the brick
fireplace when they moved.

After that we didn't pick them up.
After that we didn't hold them.
We stopped feeding the two that remained.

We expected our parents to fix them.
We expected our parents to protect
their investment.
We expected our parents to remove the bodies
while we slept.

We didn't know how to fashion our small ribs

into boats.

THE USUAL MIX OF DISMAL NEWS

Are the birds getting smaller to survive
or just getting smaller?

It is, apparently, natural for the eagle to catch the octopus
not so the other way around—that so many arms
should cling to the bird of this country.

Did the deer found swimming need saving?
And what did the men do after pulling her from the water?

The language is disquieting.

Nuna ushnertuq.[1]
Yaatiini, akgua'aq, ernerpak cali aqllangenguartuq.[2]
Arnat qutmi.[3]

So too the whales, the walrus, long-toothed, white-faced bears (who were mothers
once and after all) and wolves and—
everywhere the ice is thinning.

At which point the unusual mortality event
isn't.

---

[1] land gives way
[2] the days wind   up
[3]   women on the beach

IT'S HARD TO SIGNAL MY DISTRESS WITH HANDS
AROUND MY NECK IN EVERY DREAM

Still, I want the birds in my dream
to have been eagles
gold & white &
fighting
          if they must
but just
passing through.

I want what they dropped
from grasping claws
into
          the icing lake to have been
small & covered
in
          matted fur instead of hair tangled
like my brother's girl
or the girl they found
in Kotzebue.

I wanted to be on a lake that doesn't ice
I wanted to be in any other boat
I wanted to remember
                    how to jump
                    how to swim
                    how to remain light
on my feet
   wanted to be primed
                    to run.

All girls' hair knows how
to tangle like that
                    like mane
        or chrysalis—

want to wake full chested
with lungs large enough to make
                    waves that rise in the desert

want to be light & to be loud enough
to find you in the dark.

THE MEDIA WOULD LIKE TO TELL ME THE COLOR
OF MY FISH TAIL ON ANOTHER DAY FOR WEARING RED

Or was it my aura? Only those
who can see red
will be able to read these words.

A child walks the familiar road.
A body is found at the mile mark.
Still
    you do not suspect foul play.
Still
    you say she was Not Afraid.

You say they are not afraid,
You say we are not afraid,
You say I am not afraid,
    and because I understand the need
to maintain appearances
    and because I understand the in/
significance of my own threat/
        of disappearance

I say I am Not Afraid.

I wear only red /each day
    [another] goes missing.

I wear red and still
    you think of what to do with me
        what you'd like to do
    with us in our red dress.

Very well I will be red like a plague
    like a body/
        of water rising/
    a name held   red rising
        in the throats before
channels close.

I will be red like the mouth
    spitting fire in the Pacific.

I will be the one made m/other
    in the beginning,

        one made to break
    to scatter light to every window
-less interior

      fire spat
from the sea.

PALINODE

In conversation with the "Elimination of Innocence" triptych
by Thomas Stream

Besides unusually large amounts of dead birds
ghosts. That is,
memory of birds so thick
no sky
          of impossible angles
          of landing

memory of boats
in the water
thick with fish.

Now the girls are losing
their wings.
Now the bodies sink.
Now the river is a harbinger
          a garment grieving
          a bit of red thread
          a tangle of shine
          a wreck—

Thomas, you showed us the women
could be bird.
You showed us the women
thrown overboard
               knew how to fly
after all.

You showed us a Stream
          these days could still be
          benevolent.

This time I think we should
aim for fish, something plated
slippery & fit
for the waters to come

              something with teeth
capable of pulling their own
weight
              heavy with seed
ashore.

＾

the women buried after had shorter lives and greater stress.
the women buried after had greater stress but more prestige.
the women buried after took more silver to their prestigious graves.
the sacrificial women went with more silver to their early graves.

early to bed,

in the beginning there is always a   woman(men) & or
                                             flooding.

must the heroine be vindictive or entombed?
        the heroine is vindictive and

WAVE TROUGH. the lowest part of the wave. **the low point**

(at) the lowest point the medium sinks

WHEN YOU CAN'T THROW ALL THE MEN
INTO THE OCEAN & START OVER

The death toll from a typhoon & ensuing floods reaches 61.

The government has said some reservoirs are dangerously near
capacity after persistent rain.

The prism is a promise. Tell me, what was the last promise you kept? No sin
is committed under threat of bodily harm or a death

                                          and not to have any body
seems possible to fall / under one of those categories.

It's possible you don't know what any of this means. We're in the post-fall
month, after all.

Some capsized at sea. Others killed / in a landslide.

We're still talking about gun disease over here. Under threat of bodily harm.
Or death.

Twenty-six teenage women are found dead at sea. Officials wonder
if they were killed.

Women who cannot swim as well as men are more likely to drown. Or
women might also try to rescue their children from drowning. Women
might be penetrated by foreign objects

                                    such as men and guns.

Women might endure. We're still talking about consent over here. Do you have
all your teeth?

I am sick of this country and its guns a poet says. I am sick of this country
and its bodies.

This land too could be beautiful. I too am a thief. Seven years ago today
the white owl in my ear lost a wing.

Are you paying attention?

It's too far to pick up and go /
home.

SEA CHANGE

There was a man who set out to obtain charms.
Going out in a baidarka, he landed in the place he was heading for.

If it were me I'd put a small house on the water
with a bird to carry dry land.

And the bird would be dressed as a man.

That way when the men come for the daughters
they will simply fly away
                              and when the sons are carried
far from the sea it will be by their own beating
wings their granddaughters will find their way home.

They will say they are filling up.

They won't say the bodies are filling the sound.

They won't tell you the otters who were hunted were more
or less human
                    another time.

Common to the Gulf waters of the people of the island
that is, the island-people:

>   birds in flight
>   anadromous fish
>   three kinds of
>   sharks

[including the sleeper, perceived non-threatening. perceived
opportunistic. perceived, consumed, intoxicating.]

>   also fireweed and
>   forget-me-nots

also stone smoothed
              sinkers

and fish with faces

common fish
              with faces,

Common to the water and the people of the island
that is, as such stories go:

a girl was not harmed "by the capsizing
or by taking in water, living after that
on the bottom of the sea."

Common to the water
              as such stories go:

"if at sea something like a swaddled child appears,
we paddle to it and, passing by it, pull it out from
its wrapping and [so] get safely away."

(One plucks out its clout.)

"However, whoever flees from it will get taken by it."

⌁

In this story all the children live.
I have a great-grandmother and she lives.
I have a grandmother and she lives.
I have a daughter and she lives.
In this story I am not afraid of sleeping
waves.
In this story I am not afraid.
I am not afraid and we live.
We all live.

Each sole of my fine shoes I have torn out

and shaped into a finer boat like one

who knows how to make fine boats and give

them to one's relatives

one knows how to name

one knows how to believe

they are living

that all the children have not died and are

living still.

⌒

Qayak ang'uq.[1]
Qaik miktuq.[2]
Tununiten imami.[3]

When one is going to hold what one has held before
the bottom of one's palms itches.

He who is to walk the following day
the sole of his foot itches.

[S]he who is to have sorrow
[her] throat is full.

---

[1] a boat is a body that grows
[2] out of the squall—
[3] don't turn your back on the water (, the sea, the wave, the rising tide).

Build safer boats.

USE THAT WHICH IS FOR EMPTYING

She hears night eyes closed
sing her sleeping

water shushing rock
breaking down
the violent ends
of glass

wind she didn't cross
she never crossed
a one

the child playing hide
& seek her body
between two hard places
she is rock & she
is porous
nesting in the tall grass   where

you can't see her—unless
you look

see, this is not a game
see, we harden as we fall

the way these things go:
when a storm descends to speak
with you
You better listen / of course

you listen
you there still living—

the water's bound
to get in
to your boat

asirnituq, imanga'iyutaq aturu![1]

---

[1] it is / not well,

IF A LIABILITY OF YOUR OWN MAKING

If these dreams mean anything women who conjure fire are ambiguously dangerous then I suppose but we were the ones who let the flames grow out of hand abundant in the dark. *puyulek yakguani et'aar[ni]tut*

[(*see,*) The one down there at the bottom of the sea, the one who did not wish to marry]

I could look up what these portents mean, or have meant, but I know what you would say: I already know, and I do, and *and* we don't reduce to blood and bones in the field. or sheets

And I do know what you're going to say you're right but now we can begin again:

In a manner, it went like this

not mothers   not daughters   not sisters,
women (called whores)

not sons   not brothers   not fathers,
boys or
       the land—
which (to you) means more? I mean
which will [do you think] fetch a higher price?

These went in or through the woods and did not come out or back

These went ~~through~~ into the crooked fields   kept growing over   their mouths they outgrew (their mouths) we kept [them] unke[m]pt to hide their worth from

not neighbors   not hungry,
glutted:

      the glutted ones on every side

I tried to pull water from the fountain but silt stopped up my pail thin
necked—if the rivers are no longer running what distinguishes silt from rocks
thrown into the well but force and repetition? keep throwing rocks sooner or
later the base breaks down. or builds up. I mean these camps were pitted
against each other from the start

If this is my dream I can change it as I tell you

The water ~~had~~ has agency. ~~it~~ we could move those rocks if ~~it~~ we desired

I was running out of time the thorn-hemmed fields had grown to see what

we grew in places
we kept hidden

women not daughters and boys not fathers and land   stubborn as it was
(and shrewd)
at the current juncture—

I was running out of time:

The house was unsteady the road obscured at night

In the dark we came together with our not neighbors   the glutted ones   where
we could see
their mouths   our kid gloved hands   where their/our mouths would be
the fires glow

We let our yards burn to be sure we were all up to our necks in ash
together   (water could have stopped us at any point. shore lines would have to be
negotiated)

We couldn't keep our hair straight so we cut it close
to our heads. it became impossible to look at the others and not see sheets
were faced
by day/s

we were trying to survive. we were trying to hold our small burnt worlds we had
tilled to pass on our children and their children all while growing smaller

still

at night we came together to see for ourselves

each smaller still

I know what you mean, put it all together *and*:

The shores won't hold for long, the word of the day is volcano. *puyulek yakguani et'aar[ni]tut.*[1]

---

[1] see how we are opening, here (here, pull the string wrapping round) the neck

SIX LINES FOR CHRISTINE

He went to war
He came home
We were married.

I never asked her what she dreamed
The nights before she told me to bury her
In the dress she wore to her only son's wedding.

LETTER TO THE DAUGHTER I WOULD LIKE TO HAVE

I still wake weeping after dreams
of my grandmothers

     wonder if they would like my small dog
what they would say to the cat.

Don't ask me how the dog knows
each time I wake regardless
of my body's tendency to set hard when I think
no daughter of mine shall weep for me.

Fur fills my lungs til my own breath
won't:

Breathing is a costly act/
I wish to return
to sleep.

               ~c

My black-haired grandma didn't want to be a bother
when she felt the water rising in her lungs.

My mother's mother went into the earth in her finest
leopard self.

I want to build a boat
          a body
large enough to carry us all

these days these waters not fit for wading,
this mud hungers
              for our living.

The blood stops
in my veins
        aware of every other body at rest
and my threat to that state
of ease.

I would sooner let every particle of dust
all the dirt and salty water
seal every opening

       sooner let the fluid petrify / in
my womb than risk
awaking others, but already

           arnat qutmi et'ut[1]
           imat kuingtut[2]

we, the break in time—

---

[1] at the beach
[2] the women are waking

NOTES

ALL THE DAUGHTERS This poem borrows a line from the poem "sacrifice/circumference," by Kristin George Bagdanov, in *Fossils in the Making* (Black Ocean, 2019).

HOW IT GOES A white teenage boy at the Capitol, there to protest women's rights, wearing a red hat expressing a desire to return the country to some imagined greatness I can only imagine requires also a return to the subjugation and silencing of those minorities who have managed after nearly 250 years of this "grand experiment" in democracy to win at the very least lip service to their human dignity, smirks in the face of a tribal elder, reportedly shrugs and says "Land gets stolen, that's how it works," and somehow comes out the victim in the media. As tens of thousands march for the supposed rights of the unborn, rights that somehow cease to matter at that magical first breath, a nation that would be seen as a model to the rest of the world enacts a policy of separating the wrong kind of mothers from their already born children. The numbers are unstable from the beginning. We've always been poor at keeping records, and I can't help but think, with all the resources we pour into the bureaucracy of each small act, this ineptitude is not accidental. While I am not convinced the boy meant no harm or disrespect, I can readily believe he didn't know any better. After all, this country has fantastic powers of amnesia. After all, those tasked with distributing the news in this country either readily forget or never learned that the American military was deployed against its own citizens in 1873 and 2016. Of course, in 1873, they weren't properly counted as citizens at Wounded Knee. And both there and at Standing Rock, they were the wrong demographic to elicit sympathy. Or maybe it's fatigue. Even if accurate numbers of children separated from their parents under (and since) 45 were available, crisis fatigue has already set in, such that 215 children found buried at the sites of former residential schools in Canada jumps to 6,509 and hardly anyone is talking about it. Not even to keep the buzz north of the border so to avoid reckoning with our own longstanding and unacknowledged history of separating children from their mothers. Through massacre. Through boarding schools. (How many more will we find?) Through a child's services that disproportionately finds nonwhite mothers and their nonwhite ways of parenting inadequate so that 20,000 children are redistributed to white, mostly middle-class couples in what is now called the sixties scoop. These histories are not taught. These news stories get buried. That's how it works. Even now the state of Texas is challenging the Indigenous Child Welfare Act passed to prevent a repeat of the sixties scoop and preserve indigenous cultural and familial support in the event a child really must be removed. If this seems a strange tangent in an otherwise lyrical revisioning of violence against indigenous women and the resilience of such women in the face of that violence, you haven't been paying attention. The same narratives that facilitate violence against women facilitate violence against the landscape facilitate violence against indigenous people and other nonwhite populations. And the same hypocrisy, bureaucratic ineptitude, and cultural amnesia allow these violences to continue.

Numbers cited in this poem are from the following sources. Numbers subject to change, have already changed.

Number of migrant children forcibly separated from their parents at the southern border under the administration of 45: www.usatoday.com/story /news/politics/2019/01/17/hhs-inspector-general-family-separations/ 2603282002/

Number of immigrant children held in U.S. detention centers: www.cnn.com/2018/11/23/politics/hhs-record-14000-immigrant-children -us-custody/index.html

Number of children buried at the Carlisle Indian School, number of children separated from their families to attend the Carlisle Indian School; (in the nineteenth and twentieth centuries, there were 60, 106, or 350 government- funded Indian boarding schools): carlisleindianschoolproject.com/past/

Number of missing and murdered indigenous women and girls, prone to be incorrectly labeled (and undercounted): nonprofitquarterly.org/2018/11/21 /a-new-study-on-missing-and-murdered-indigenous-women-and-girls -highlights-challenges/

Number of Alutiiq people, mostly women and children, massacred by Shelikhov in an "extreme case" of "self-defense" when they refused to turn over hostages and trade the furs on which they depended to buyers in China: www.independent.co.uk/news/long_reads/native-american-women-missing -murder-mmiw-inquiry-canada-us-violence-indigenous-a8487976.html

Alternatively, such facts vary—by the time you read this we will have forgotten how many. The list grows. But who's counting?

I TOO GROW TIRED OF THE PLOT This poem is in conversation with the poem "In the Middle of the Myth," by Taije Silverman.

PALINODE This poem references the "Elimination of Innocence" triptych (gouache on paper) by the Unangan painter Thomas Stream. The Stonington Gallery website provides Stream's account of the massacre:

> Early in 1762, Aleuts on Unga Island near the Alaska mainland responded to Russian assaults on their women by carrying out attacks that killed eight traders and wounded several more. The surviving Russians fled, returning to Siberia with a cargo of 900 sea otter pelts and 25 young Aleut girls, who met with a cruel fate.
>
> When the ship reached the coast of Siberia, armed Russians escorted 14 of the girls ashore to pick berries. Two of them managed to escape, and an enraged officer then killed another girl on the spot. This so upset the rest of the girls that they jumped from the boat carrying them back to the ship and drowned. Unnerved, the Russian officer tried to eliminate all trace of the incident by ordering the remaining Aleut girls who had stayed on the ship thrown overboard. The crime later surfaced during an inquest into the abuses of the trading company that sponsored the journey.

From this terrible story Stream has conjured beauty: a triptych honoring the murdered women that shows their spirits transformed into birds.

ACKNOWLEDGMENTS

Thank you, as always, to my incredible support system, my husband Daniel, my family, my mentors, my friends.

Thank you to the Caldera Arts Residency Program in Sisters, Oregon; the Wrangell Mountains Center in McCarthy, Alaska; and Elsewhere Studios in Paonia, Colorado, for the gift of time, space, and kindred spirits as this work unfolded.

Thank you to my Colorado cohort: Katie, Melissa, Cedar, and Catie, for your care with this work.

And, of course, thank you to the wonderfully attentive team at Wesleyan University Press, and especially Suzanna Tamminen for her keen editorial guidance.

Poems from this collection first appeared in the beautiful pages of these generous journals:

"Letter to the Daughter I Would Have Liked to Have," "When You Say the Deer Swept Out to Sea Was 'Saved,'" and "I Too Grow Tired of the Plot" in *The Capilano Review* (Summer 2021)

"How About a Unicorn Horn?" [as "A Prong or Sharp Point, Such as That on a Fork, or an Antler"], "A Persistent Dream of Large Bodies" [as "A Persistent Dream of Large Bodies of Water & Everything That Might Be Waiting Within"], and "A Four-Part Apology for My Continued Being" in *Grub Street* (Spring 2021)

"She Is Making Rope," and "*Uriitarsurciqua*," in *Ariel-Art*, vol. 2 (2020); ariel-art.com/chabitnoy-vol_2

"The Media Would Like to Tell Me the Color of My Fish Tail on Another Day for Wearing Red" [as "Girls Are Coming Out of the Water," winner of the 2021 Anne Halley Poetry Prize] in *The Massachusetts Review* (Winter 2020)

"In the Field," "Holes in the Field," and "Six Lines for Christine" in *Peripheries 3* (August 2020)

"If You're Going to Look Like a Wolf They Have to Love You More than They Fear You" in Poem-a-Day (November 4, 2019); poets.org/poem/if-youre-going-look-wolf-they-have-love-you-more-they-fear-you-0

"Palinode" in *Poetry Northwest* (February 2020); www.poetrynw.org/abigail
 -chabitnoy-three-poems/

"Baptism by Fire" and "How It Goes" in *Texas Review* (2019)

"Anatomy of a Wave" and "In the Current Where Drowning Is Beautiful" in
 "New Poetry by Indigenous Women," a series curated by Natalie Diaz on
 LitHub (2018); lithub.com/new-poetry-by-indigenous-women-3/

"Camouflage, Defense, and Predation Being Among the Reasons" in *The Pinch*
 (2018)

"Signs You Are Standing at the End," in *What Nature*, a *Boston Review*
 anthology (2018)

"Sea Change" [as "Sea Change, Heavy from the West"] in *The Map Is Not the
 Territory*; themapisnot.com/issue-12-abigail-chabitnoy

ABOUT THE AUTHOR

Abigail Chabitnoy is the author of *How to Dress a Fish* (Wesleyan 2019), winner of the 2020 Colorado Book Award for Poetry and shortlisted in the international category of the 2020 Griffin Prize for Poetry. Her poems have appeared in *Hayden's Ferry Review*, *Boston Review*, *Tin House*, *Gulf Coast*, *LitHub*, and *Red Ink*, among others. She was a 2016 Peripheral Poets fellow, the 2020 recipient of the Indigenous Poet Residency at Elsewhere Studios in Paonia, Colorado, supported by the Witter Bynner Foundation, and is a mentor for the Institute of American Indian Arts MFA in Creative Writing. Abigail is a Koniag descendant and member of the Tangirnaq Native Village in Kodiak, Alaska. She holds a BA in anthropology and English from Saint Vincent College in Latrobe, Pennsylvania, and an MFA in creative writing from Colorado State University in Fort Collins, Colorado.